Delay

POETS
OUT LOUD

Elisabeth Frost, *series editor*

The Hello
Delay

Julie Choffel

Fordham
University Press
New York
2012

Fordham University Press has no
responsibility for the persistence or
accuracy of URLs for external or
third-party Internet websites referred
to in this publication and does not
guarantee that any content on such
websites is, or will remain, accurate
or appropriate.

Fordham University Press also
publishes its books in a variety of
electronic formats. Some content
that appears in print may not be
available in electronic books.

Library of Congress Cataloging-in-Publication Data
is available from the publisher.

Printed in the United States of America
14 13 12   5 4 3 2 1
First edition

For Mom, Dad, Suzanna, and Lizzie

and the worlds we inhabit separately

and together

Contents

Is everything that happens
something else again. And
what do we call that.

—Mary Burger, from
The Boy Who Could Fly

Serenade, or After Others

Here, from a fake rose
I've made you a real one

my poetry has no camera

The holes between the stars and the holes the stars
will leave in the sky

Cardinal Sketch

Rough and literate, your bits make a cheery piece:
to try windows / to grate one's teeth.

Keep placidly along the lines
of droll translation. Not merely a hat of polite passage,
but a rimmed ottoman and a sitter
or glass of burgundy with friend.

Lukewarm, I knew it. Infused air *is* your body;

happy campers abound in these parts.
Your gray self is more of an other.
Please fill to the top. And until there is something else to say.

Table – Chair – Toy

the top of joy – this smell – a cloud forest – assist us in concentrating – even clanging comes from somewhere – darling, ling – an amount of supper spreads out – the cat paws a pleistocene crumb under one's house – a modern phone call between meals knows details of your name – mice swarm to have their day – another doubtful fantasy – drag a weighted fork – the tools await in the shed featherlight and faithful – a time machine in misty smoke reminisces – trick or treat – juvenile breathing, cautionary tales, incomplete phrasing – easy compositions all around

Menagerie – Scenery – Suburb

daily measure the trunk how grown – begin the race of trees –
down the street the last store to sell ice cream wins a heart –
forgetting the bear in the park – yes, find another – milk drips
from the leaves or shapes of leaves – puddles gather on lawns
– an aunt appears before her lineage with message – how to
tell time – how to flail out of a tree in frustration – flail then
wring leaves dry – the old quarters shining in the sun – chil-
dren's music floats on pavement and want – upheld like a
working pony – necessarily superfluous – the let down – a
switch to – an eight p.m. summer lung – the coded oak sleepy
and silly – milk the tree for the time being

Heart – Code – Home

built into the trail – privacy's feeble dugout – a pantry's selec-
tion of fruits – disintegrated very much as in small bones –
negative capability sees only short distances – imagine a grand
scaling of ant paths – almost gestures toward – the furthest toe
showing in the sandal – end edge of pattern – purling morning
toward later – swishy limbs – escaping a surface – almost in
the sky – autobiography of biplane – a seat in the bird – a trap
in the word – a lean-to

Sinkhole – Sunspot – Parasol

vitamin mineral ink – terraced subterranean asleep on top –
mange in a patchy pelt – the smelter cooler painters move in –
whose lane is longest with cypresses shifting – indifference to
the general pleasure – a mule haunts tunnels looking for a
spark – in the air by now – that billow above cactus – a hun-
dred-year bloom – metallics still booming – and want of vein
or layer – pattern smarts in the hummingbird quick – in the
early birds and sculpture salons – the pretend saloon – we bear
the sight – canyon towns their outcast clay – key to the drive-
way in concrete – cheeking creek side – run down the sparkling
cross-section of cover – a part of the sun come down – an offer
opposite pearl

Snowman – Motor – Mammal

neverland's nevermind – running up through ground to ground level – cascade backwards and artesian – the topical, psychotropic battle – grinding spices to achoo – taking the runway – to cliffs of divers in the ice capades – let's make scores from scratch – finalizing scenes – to the go-between – to the haberdashery – the upper hand – underground – dear pumpkin – a deer runs after a vegetable – a slow-down in stead of cop-out or show-off – variously an herbivore – a bulletin of grocery goods in reverse – but first a barrel of omnivores

The Rain Falls as a Cylinder

Inside the bamboo lifestyle
mud is paper mud
the sky has creases in it
split-level shelves suspend
onion-skin windows

if you have a parchment bundle
you have got to take its picture

once the only leaved tree looks like an uncrimping
butterfly

get you to moving books by the page
bringing in the mailbox
in the letters:
keep up the mud
the stained-glass sun
the pinecone firehouse
the cornered eyesight
ball of plain yarn tenting itself
       (pelt it was)

Synopsis

I

Someone is on the phone and its voice is the inner marble.
She is like her voice is and like the statements
she is making in a bowl
not "howling"
or "timing herself"
with her capacities like like like sly telephones

A drawer falls out of the chest like a dark lantern
Rules remember themselves in a vacuum

"The room was filled up"
And one wanted to be a friend
talked of this like we talk of filling up houses

Granted
no one has talked of mice
or sand or milk or zinnias or lead paint poisoning

but someone was "on the phone" and continues
using pronouns like disasters
(what if we don't stop)

2

That burliness comes from burls, if it does, and that
                                significance
from signifiers like "that"
she knows these things and is on the phone anyway

remembering the outer marble is difficult
when we have all of these ideas

The stuff falls out of the stuff
The rain falls as a fodder
and hybrid "for the most part"

Talking about how to make resilient boxes we talk about
                               redwoods
do they stand for themselves like women
and are they alive like a self or a family or a farmer's market
and how many of them touch up there

3

Please dial slowly
I would like to speak in "hierarchies of thought"
to the buildings the marble is passing through

"passing" is sad enough
though, on top of that, the line has an echo
like a physical movement

waving back
Hello matter of course

Hello, reasonable delay

Hello, tried-and-true

Hello, falling market value

Hello, lonely cartwheel

Hello, gathering portholes

Hello, sincerest garden variety

Hello, massacre of the perfection of snails

Plant Life

Gestalt of a flowering
reminds me
taken aback

by the cochineal or wavery oat

my oar is in the water, also
that plantlife
who else

      'nobody knows
      the trouble I've seen'

an outcrop, a cropping, crow
and we're clapping

and maybe we're making what we desire
are you that marathon

plantlife runs up to me
wish swish wish

there's a story & a girl herbalist
she goes for the ones she knows
she knows them all differently
which makes it more complicated
than the story

     (fountains of pattern)
the birds are up and down

we keep going if it seems familiar
the mallow opens its faces
we kneel in the bedtime evening
the wildflowers are wilder than us

nobody knows if nothingness has a form
but should it come, would we each know it
or would it be our lack of knowledge

take shelter in plantlife
la la la

this is not what it was supposed to
(put the sun away)
we think the words that intend us
all brides-to-be
& jacks-in-the-pulpit

      'glory' &
          'hallelujah'

ha, ha, ha, ha,
the plantlife breathes
like karate
      into all my old
nudges

      kiln-builder
      press-forger
      silkworm-grower
scene-maker,
associating facts with pleasure
      the fern grows like a tree

except when stunted
        and then it just grows
all come-what-may

(do you have a favorite
        yes)
(is there time for you to say it
        no)

will the plantlife wait for us
always
maybe

heltery-skeltery
comes a-tripping
        here's coxcomb, brainflower
and alpine dwarves, winter incubators

weather's containment
        could pluralize us too, like life life life
in a fallout shelter

without us, plantlife absorbs all the foggy days
takes back the side/walks—

        'one, two,
skip to my lou,
three, four,'
memory fails the important phrases

the brushy creeks
hollow trails

scrappy oaks
& filler life, & filler decease

and this is where you disappear
is where you're filtered into a future,
bending slantwise and able
to make food from light
but doubtfully capable of feeling blue

is sound my blue culpability, now, song,
sung, sang, sing,
formed from fringes
my hair or the passion vine

twiddling our thumbs
          'hey hey, alright, hey hey'
winter is coming, & fall first
the plantlife measures
longer & shorter

harvesting, we catch the sunrise
ask whose domesticity
the sun has

this many years coming down
each night
          children anchored
in its arms, facing the pregnant
datura—
I am full, full
are you ready, are you ready
hey – old – rock – steady

constant as opuntia, more seasoned than a sycamore
I am no more surprised than the grass
raising its back

the funny days are upon us
& we're
entertained by walking
messing it all up
  'When I say Go, you say Animal!'
  Go . . .

one uses seaweed to make her nest on land

another whistles to match the hemisphere
  (watch that correspondence)
nothing adds up except piles of seeing & hearing
these orders

I get up with the sun now
to take a peek

spores in the skies my memorabilia
whose purpose having fled
be the skies falling anew

and then down (don't forget) into the sweet, sweet biomes
to live to
make some background

and my cheek
rolls down against the
quiet, busy waters
working the veins

Mindful Or

"raising the eyes" "softening the neck"
distract a static body with
first the low-fi syncopation of the lungs
then any small motion

but nothing to write home about.
Dear Home: I have seen it all and I know the graduation of
                                                              birds
to the clock's front porch is all hope and farce

you wish you could be an actualized time
like a swath of colors in the sky *before* rain

instead you are instead

"do you believe in what you see"
filter girl, conditional gal
"all that" and more

lifting the leg, there's a bar.
"what more might we ask" of ourselves after
imagination,
Dear First Base: Can you come home with me.

Something Must Be Described

I was looking through the window from out of it, able to see in and through to the other window where it was sunny out and a cloud.

Look, I was a small and painfully bright finch. You might say I was thumb-sized.

Someone was walking along the other side of our door, when, and then you said if she was real we would have known her.

Sometimes the canon of information eludes me. I want it all. Always soon as I want everything I'm done with wanting for a while. Wishy-washy like that. Sometimes the very very very is unnerving, you know how we are with looking. It's another way so then why own it.

The glorious sun over the pondish lake turning into a shape, it's the first thing, and the finicky noticing. The away.

It keeps it up. There, there—spread of land is mouth and eye. I want to describe it for you.

The Lighting

The light flickers, lightly as cardboard and stiff as a spine

light passes through though it's already light out
and lights out though city litebrites shine on and persuade
                                        some to wake

though the little stars aren't all what they seem and the birds
                                        are not
all reptile, though vermin wait until dark they see it lightly
great blankets cover the highways and homing pigeons go on
anyway

everyone's for or against the light

none of the lights are false
as they access greater light
they are inspired

great lights come on spherical and religious
and common
reduced they come to pinheads through eyed needles
veined and thorough
a seeping light gets into light sleep and some go blind in the
                                        daytime
and some go blind across larger fields than days and some
                                        regain their sights
and some surfaces hit some miss

a liking to mica we are layered by light and through layers we

                                                                            are

sums of the winters we have waited for its

tissue connective, free stuffing as in space, the positivity

that comes from behind things and makes them vague

The Beauties

The beauty is in your mouth where all things are
the beauty falls down and over your face
the beauty is dragon-like in air
and knows you are not a corpse
or a moon
and the beauty knows how to tell between grape juice and apple
and its beauty is of the beauties that are velvet, slightly warm,
and anticipating
when you look out of windows, or through great vines taking
over orchards
like a beauty plague
and pages and pages written in other languages to call it out of
this language
and one's longing for it means one will never truly see it but
in passing
as the injured hobble near it, the pale rub against it, and the
beauty still prepares you
for other beauty, not exactly like anything in this one but by
name
so you might continue looking at it like anything else not
wholly undertaken
and those who walk near you may begin to bear witness to your
witness
the beauty pausing briefly, just a pulse, and forgetful.

How You Do

My sisters and your layer cakes
you-hoos and formal
introductions,
enchanté, glissade, my country
how many yous do I have to choose from
each of your eyelashes
sweeping under nightlight shade
you, who go to bed each night

you who are taking the bed ruffles with you
when you go

going strong in the project for justice
and plenty
skating by in the moonlight with milk

you of coming back, of foreign diplomacy,
afterthoughts, past you
beloved you singing in pine trees

you of languages and forfeited meanings
you of your mindset
        (. . . this song is about you)
           you bet, you think
revised you

your self-portrait
feminine you said by a woman

you forcing flowers before the spring because
you can't wait, you without precedent
you in coats and slightly contagious

forgiving the strangers
who can't find your address
as you haven't been numbers since cheering

form of you in snow and man, formal and casual
you, pink under suburban light, citrine near the urban
criminal you

fake you
formality you
fleeting you

your boredom overhauling the poolside,
icing your water, pushing the sailboats off to float

your silly

fabulist cherry tree you growing rubies, fingering
sunlight, trappist monkish you praying and drinking
saddened by the forfeit
of historical yous

transdisciplinary you between symbols
you made of twine from the ever-useful yucca
you who act like a dancer in russia
        spinning inward quickly, outward slow

a glass canary
oscillating glances
midway you in the fanning pattern
sprinkling feelings across the grass

Producing for a While

I think I'm done with producing for a while. I know I can contribute a lot to the overall production. But I'm done with producing until I can get some input. They said, if we produce you, you sign a contract. If you sign our contract, we will feed you an extra meal per day. If you don't want this extra meal, you cannot give it away to someone else without a contract. If you produce meals spontaneously, we can not be responsible for your production. I said I think I'm done. They said give us a break I said give me a break. We broke everything together and it was useful for me. I needed some input for my overall worth and so they contributed. I had to admit that I wanted them to produce me. I had to fulfill the terms. The terms said I was done producing for a while. They produced a document that said I would show them my terms. I thought when I get enough input I'll show them. I showed them what I knew about production by waiting it out. They said what if we gave you more input. I said you don't get it I think I'm done with producing for a while.

The Sorrows

We will continue
this later

I don't know how to be any more forthcoming than this
in the "everyone crying" scene
too close to the sound the highway makes
so our own busy music whinnies aside
is sore

in the "everyone looks elsewhere" scene
I can only see my own eyes
seeking their place

in how the present sorrows us, overheard
in the late-night pancake house
where you still get one pancake
and one egg
and one bacon slice for two dollars
while you sip the multiple coffee to keep not dreaming of the
overlapping

to make the dreams come in the wake
and avoid the soft
you love

and unlike proper affirmations, they gleam a gray gleam, like
halls

appearing as nineteen-story windows, appearing as birds of

                                                       prey

and the sorrows fall into your lap, animals
downy and sharp, cross-eyed at first

and these are not your mother's sorrows but those your father

                                    warned you about

saying, "these are the sorrows I have placed in the boat"
saying, "these are without destination, as all vertical places

                                          exist,"

and the light throws you a stone

and the pebbles collect in your gut along the sad line of the

                                          timeline

the sand is never real sand, but some uncatapultable feeling of

                                          sand

and everyone is there.
Suddenly, everyone is there and so is the light, retracting the

                                          first stone,

and the sorrows speak to tell, tell to story,
story to continue, pretty please.

Exposure Story

"and the nightingale" "and your breath"
      and your slow-motion ticking
leave us justified, sitting again
but not like babies who just learned
to sit up

and the flicker of the ticker-tape
like leaves moving singly on trees
lingering,
      "you take care now"

and "I'm going to the Spanish corner"
what's that

you say there are not enough lanterns in a Spanish night
Spain does not like breakfast
"enough"

the highlights are graduating up the hillside
and we are reversible liars
like you have come inside every night, "in your life"

and nobody likes you enough.
"never be like the sun," or was it
"I'll never"? we need to hike around to find
the paper trail.
you just didn't know what trilling meant,

      "how could you" not know
what I'm saying
especially when the sun comes up and I'm singing it

Post Script

for Pallavi Sharma Dixit

As you continue floating down and out the sky for always;
    as I forgo my duties that I might foresee instead.
As you wear things which are orange or righteous;
    as I wear things which are soft and culpable.
As you prepare meals by which to glean light;
    as I eat like a child with a game on my face.
As you wonder why rain comes in packs
    as I stumble over you as an essential word

What is the recognizable form
What is the recognizable form
What is the recognizable form

As the messenger negates the idea of angels
    we love him for it

As gazing and intentional as men
    but false in this also

What is the recognizable form

In the sentry house where the sentry sleeps

In the pretense of glory

Hidden in a mesh of stars or happening like knowledge of the
    name of a melody

Hating the word growth

Sending (you send me)

Inalienable (the awesome)

What is the recognizable (from)

Ahead, to the past
futures ticked off the fence line

Whorishly (available)

Garishly (present)

Absolutely (platonic)

Whether to capitalize
on this

What is recognizable (what)

If Anything

If people can't be what they want

no one's going to become a specialized bird
that uses its beak to
finger a way through the waters
everything's of

the clues that you have a soul
you make imaginary
and natural as nature, everything seeking
what's regal but reality's this
antithesis,

action quickens for action to persevere
people sing without mics
lots of them sing along separately at the same time
wherever the radio goes
and later on they eat real food

synthesizing the limes in their tea with the harmonic octave

                                                          they
squish these actions together
they know how to do this and they do more than this because
they can do this in their sleep

The Debriefing

the sound was shabby with age
my family had gone home
you asked me to see the fish out of the water
and other acts of kindness
and other acts

where I saw it flapping in the wind

I threw it into air that was carrying on

when I heard changing its rhythm

where the thing stalled its dying

where nothing just died in the stale sun

in the gallery-facing windows

she was a silver fish while

all gold ones are solemn

and how the whereabouts had more sensitivity to direction
than they

when each life was meaningful, in grapelike cluster

with the qualities of elapse and unsudden drift

ascent got too far connotated

to say summer is coming

to say mother is keening

with all possible others

for to bring heavier pleasure to the table

laying down the cloth

give your hands to the gods

give your hands unlike x

so many ways of not knowing what

there is not a word, knowing what words it isn't, yet

selected like everything in brevity

This World Is the Other World

You've just realized yourself and
who you are is floribunda. Some whorl sunk in a glitch.
Beanstalk, hither up, we're giddy. Fortuna, detour, fleur-de-lis.
Figures.

We said these things differently.

Ghostgirl sends her flowers.

The magnificent stream. Magnanimous flotsam
departs excessively, departs here and now, departs
futuristically.

Departs back too
　　　　(always a too).

Look it up, diction it
　　　the rune-y rules in foam of oldschool fountain drink
youthful knowledge
swimming with nonbelieving amoebae,
fabulii.

And more to "knowing": grant its collections to the needy,
pictures going up and down on the wall,
interchangeable streetcorners,
                    meanwhile galloping galloping India.

Fortuna fortuna islander, a skyscraper rooted in
causality several ways, different from the
churchbells   (pleasing affect,
naivety spontaneously combusting yer elders,
yer syntactical defense)

So much for (gracious)
vision, its long tresses motioning
toward nothingness, so much for nothing
          and ness.
                    Gorgeousing
is an easy alien

on the planet

Yer an educated planet and "you are" is
so incomplete when faced with
other planets, foggy
foggy comfort in the stars, figures in a surplus

The foreign mechanism running Burtonesque in Icelandic,

volcanic,

magenta. "What recipe"

Yer audible cipher lends a finger
to task

Unloads the leaded pencil
        (writes "penicillin")

Uncertain animal

Swear by a good lie, the lie of goodness, the lying-down lay
of inconceivable likeliness, to the good in it
to the tooth
in the dream
and its crevice

Sire an imaginative response: two-legged or not,
your concept. Someone's dotting
the you-are-heres, see-you-laters. Flittering the tummies.
Cogs get cogging and the string pulls
out

We said these things at the same time they were dissonant
we siphoned the sounds
watched their directions and just split

Part Golden, Part Hidden

Forage my language, partner.
Forsythia is tired of poetry
I am full of my own
idealized forms, that's why I could never grow
anything up north. Schizandra berry and bitter melon salad,
other people's goods. Go on your own limb
like you want it so bad
and no one gives it up
or looks you in the eye.

& if you were disguised as a pile of weeds, if you were exotic.
But the forces of nature aren't soliloquies.
"Betty went down there, well she did and she didn't"

& the murmuring delicacies at the end
of statements or scenery never complete what they set out to
                                                            say
never mend the raiment while it's being worn, being and worn

& these soft verbs and accessories, like a footbridge caught
on its foot; please dangle at your own leisure.
Please, this train is gone. Please, jumping will shift your
                                                location
just so. Think in terms of.

& my leisure *is* unhemmed, and I'm going to be
the next big gardener. Don't ask for plans, for rhythm. Ask me
where the living is.

Forthrightly and So, or Don't You Know It

Today's calculations
laden with the daffodils of the dead,
and tomorrow's flowers lie like tales.
Lay like wood.
Engrave your arms by caressing
the least safe thing you find

"your life"
(just like your life)
has no assailable edges, no ties
your dress swings on its hook
meanwhile, everything swings on its

    "everything is a smashing beauty" (too obvious)
and punches its card.
        There will be no little
unplanned babies
    in the swimming pool.
We will get the ladder out when fixing the lights.
We will be sneaky when we are called whores.

Can I Be a Part of Your We

Can I be a part of your me
Can I be a serial weevil in this book
       Can an airspace reserve a spot for the
wooing?

Can someone have a soda with herself?
My kisses are very brightly
on my mouth.   "Magnetic Field" is not the same
       as "Fielding Magnetism"
when people are made to do a thing and
when people are made
and into things.
The into is personally
excited for another person, not but simply
       "I have met a person" (a people)

and she is my difference.
The sums of humans walking around each other
are indifferent to their sameness. Hey, magnets
do not notice either. It's avoidance or collision. It's super-
sonic, hyperbolic, rhyming or using separate
straws. The one
thing I can be for sure is droll,
the one thing another can seem is pell-mell.

Don't you know someone when they begin to ask
of you things? Can you secure a thought I thought
Can y'all be a party Can I be conversations Can we

sustain "ourselves"   which
                    part will you take in
of the hum?
Your kisses are very bright
in comparison.

Beside Ourselves

"Outside my home, I like many things too."
—*Kate Bernheimer*

The plan of attack includes running
toward the oppressor until the oppressor is dead
tired. "I never get tired."

"I always wear a fanny pack for safety."
Be prepared for anything; sunburn, dogs, religion.
A ponytail encourages grabbing. Fairy
dust just works on vision, among those of us wanting
to be seen as fossilized and pure. "These sheets need
washing." "Meet me at the hottest laundromat."

"I have some great pictures of home."
Dressed up like a glam star. Worn out around
the eyes. Played again like a harmonium around the eager
                                                        hearths
of winter's edges.

"It's your house." Then my house it is.
My walk-in to another temporary.
That house resembles a mechanical scarab
feeding on mouthfuls of grass. St. Augustine,
"Only I was healthfully distracted and dying,"
"not knowing what good thing I was shortly to become."

The lounger is most useful when meaninglessness
is pleasant. "When will it come down out of the sky?"

When the symbols start assembling I'll start
to come in.

Public Service Announcement

Have you come around to listening to
the sound of your own voice recorded:
When messages repeat they delay their messages;
when messages delete they're afterwards fixed
in time; how then the play commences.

The commentators keep telling the same stories about what
you saw
when you saw specifics in their generalizations.
How the salty voices of the common people were really just
salt.
The green room, writers with objects,
the future, alternately filled and emptied,
the faucets running like a cautionary tale.

If I could have all of the naps I would not take them;
I would give some away to some people I know.
Because people say they are tired but tired
is temporary, though real; tired is save-it-for-later, the real is
tired.

You made the message but then it runs off.

The catalogue arrives, filled to the brim with tongue and wage.
"Careful with water," she sings, "careful with salt."
And we lower ourselves into the fabric
of familiar hills someone once told us about,
those we once knew of, those we now know.

If Everyone Came to Me

and how I might feed them. would we invent a dinner, improv a sleepover? if everyone awoke for breakfast. and everyone had an orange. this coming to.

if everyone dove into a river when the siren goes off. if, once wetted, we appeared in the vicinity of that which we marry. grew all flowers bigger than dahlias and built all effects out of these. and once out of flowers, used fake ones. sanctioned the struggle between the two and watched them battle it out.

and when the nightingale comes to our playing of its music, and when it turns its back to everyone and shatters into ten thousand shards of nightingale, and when we turn ourselves over, do we receive these shards.

Who Doesn't Want

to be the geographer? measuring snowstorms, timing the
kairos.

hither to thither—I get schooled when I try to elaborate. my
voice out of those crevasses. she said well I never and I shan't.
and what is this sense, what's on the divining end?

eating candy, I said what I would give. the pavement rippled
itself smooth again. she gave up.

seventy pesos will ride you to your destination; you'll actually
be sorry you didn't pay more; you would have traded the names
of places not known here for the other ride. a soft sand crosses
the air. if you were god, and nothing was different.

what then, when the sun is a newer parade. there's something
spent to everything. the sky is baking powder, gun powder,
blue lake number one. I've never had a photogenic memory. I
mean, the map of all possibilities.

I Was Asking

whose happiness I had; if it was now mine to keep.

were I more than the silhouette of my prop, that I would be grateful and forthwith. and that we would be pleased and still searching. that we make shapes in each other.

this wasn't to be about complement. any accidental verisimilitudes were left to party it out. the water and the ferry, for example. they supplied us with transfers. when I swim I am running.

like a cormorant, it came my turn to come up. to respond that I was nobody's baby – only faces held me – and I inhabited their answers. my come-on, singing my up-and-away song.

part of the kite made a line in my hand; my line fills that one when its shape is endangered.

I Will Whisper

it to you so that someone else may hear it. whether or not it's heard by you, whether or not I hear it myself—that it is heard by a stranger.

stranger and stranger. get out the fires and fire hoses, put away the stars. daybreak breaks into noon breaks into after, and after is a song, and singing makes you calmer. that's okay but what are they saying down the street and lost on you, lost on you, lost on you.

this neighborhood wants to know me through architecture and I will draw it but not with epiphany. the homeless know everything about me.

the deer lean in to listen. they can hear fire with those perfect ears. its brand new song and unmeant words, our singed houses, what anyone will say about them.

Lay Down Some Tracks

Time to open the hotel.
gain a rest. resting the peoples.

For the girl to get into the bed.
an octopus wonders how to
lay itself down. sudden beauty, stop.
sudden changing light, stop.

Gorgeous morning, character waiting
behind curtain, I don't want you anymore.
if you're such a vine why don't you appreciate the shady parts.

You're the words of the place, netting stuck in a tree.
and a big sister. heavy thing
the wind picked up, stop. springtime pop-culture tourist;
enter open room. she chooses to sleep in.
get up or stop and get up or stall
your eyes your closed ones.

Your closed ones sentient being called to. enter the
right thing. gain the fake night mind.

Afterword

Mei-mei Berssenbrugge

It was my pleasure to read Julie Choffel's rich and dimensional poems in *The Hello Delay*. I kept thinking of the opposing terms "plain" and "fancy" as applied to American folk art. The poet uses domestic words that are contemporary but echo with women's experience *as if* from the past. There are plants, fabric, food, early telephones, parchment, "vitamin mineral ink." She gathers the words into transparent, alive, and crystalline phrases—windows—and then uses these phrases like a sculptor to accrete spiritual and deep felt narratives, I want to say narrative plaints. Each phrase is a facet in a cubism that is not visual but phenomenological out of daily life. Phrases accrete in elevated abstraction. Story is partly her subject and partly her means, including story and back story, lyric extension, domestic proposal and spiritual fervor. Beautiful poems are passionate with a contained passion that tempers to the resonance of *strong* beauty:

"Here, from a fake rose
I've made you a real one

my poetry has no camera

The holes between the stars and the holes the stars
will leave in the sky." (page 3)

Notes and Acknowledgments

Many thanks to the journals in which the following poems first appeared:

27 Rue de fleures, "Part Golden, Part Hidden" and "The
  Debriefing"
American Letters & Commentary, "Beside Ourselves"
aPlod, "Mindful Or" and "If Anything"
Art New England, "Exposure Story" and "Lay Down Some
  Tracks"
Bird Dog, "If Everyone Came to Me," "Who Doesn't Want,"
  and "I Was Asking"
Caketrain, "Something Must Be Described"
Denver Quarterly, "The Sorrows" and "Synopsis"
GlitterPony, "How You Do" and "The Lighting"
Make/shift, "Producing For A While"
Mrs. Maybe, "Can I Be a Part of Your We"
The Tiny, "Table – Chair – Toy," "Heart – Code – Home," and
  "Menagerie – Scenery – Suburb"

"This World Is The Other World" first appeared in the chap-
book *Figures In A Surplus*, which was published by Achiote
Press. The title phrase comes from Robert Hass's essay "Some
Notes on the San Francisco Bay Area as a Culture Region: A
Memoir."

Some of the lines in "Serenade, or After Others," are my re-
writes of lines from James Schuyler ("Here, just for you, is a
rose made out of a real rose") and Amiri Baraka ("And now,

each night I count the stars, // And when they will not come to be counted, / I count the holes they leave").

The title "Can I Be a Part of Your We" corresponds to the line "I am part of a we and then not part of a we" in Juliana Spahr's *Fuck You—Aloha—I Love You.*

The epigraph in "Beside Ourselves" is from Kate Bernheimer's *The Complete Tales of Ketzia Gold.* St. Augustine's lines are from his *Confessions.*

This book owes much to those who heard all or some of it along the way. I am deeply grateful to Peter Gizzi and Jared Stanley for your thoughtful reading of my work; to Elisabeth Frost and everyone at Fordham for your support and guidance of this book; to Mei-mei Berssenbrugge for selecting my manuscript; and to my family, as always, for your unceasing encouragement. And to Jason, for everything between the cactus and the Cora.